On the Edge
of the Wind

Also by Linda Principe

Poetry
Tangible Remains
Echoes of Light

Nonfiction
Surviving Murder

On the Edge of the Wind

NEW POEMS

Linda Principe

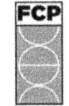

Full Court Press
Englewood Cliffs, New Jersey

First Edition

Copyright © 2020 by Linda Principe

All rights reserved. No part of this book may be reproduced or transmitted in any form or by any means electronic or mechanical, including by photocopying, by recording, or by any information storage and retrieval system, without the express permission of the author, except where permitted by law.

Published in the United States of America
by Full Court Press, 601 Palisade Avenue,
Englewood Cliffs, NJ 07632
fullcourtpress.com

ISBN 978-1-946989-81-9
Library of Congress Control No. 2020920557

Editing and book design by Barry Sheinkopf

Cover art and author photo by Debbie Mazzei

For Debbie

*who keeps me, always, from falling
off the edge of the wind and the world,
with love and gratitude*

*"Live your questions now and, perhaps,
even without knowing it, you will live along
some distant day into your answers."*
—Rainer Maria Rilke,
Letters to a Young Poet

Foreword

I cannot pretend to account for time's swift passage, and it is hard to believe it's been five years since the publication of *Echoes of Light*, nine since *Tangible Remains*. When I look in the mirror, I know where the time went, the gray in my hair a history not written in ink but there all the same. My life's changed in a multitude of ways—these last few years, in particular, some of the most challenging I've ever known. The death of my mother, the last of my immediate family, marked the end of life as I knew it, the final chapter of one existence and the birth of an entirely new one, this reinvention of myself unlike any of the others life has demanded of me.

I have now begun the part of my journey I was destined for, all my obligations fulfilled, no one to answer to or for but myself, and so, here I am.

As I write this, we are in the midst of a terrible but significant moment in history—a pandemic that's utterly decimated our sense of normalcy and awakened us to the slender thread we hang by, crime rates soaring around the country, divisiveness and hatred in every direction that feels almost inescapable. Almost. In Japanese culture, *kintsukuroi* is an ancient practice of repairing pottery and ceramic objects. In a nutshell, the cracks are filled with gold (sometimes silver or platinum, as well). The idea is that the imperfections, the fractures, become part of the visible history of the object, thus leading to the belief that something is, actually, "more beautiful for having been broken." What a perfect metaphor for the here and now.

We live in a broken world, and the words on these pages are the gold I have used to make of those fractures something enduring, a reminder that, in spite of my broken places, wholeness is possible for each of us, if we seek it. The only wasted experience is the one we fail to learn from. My greatest hope, as you approach these pages, is that you find, in my journey towards healing and harmony, pieces of your own; and may you see and acknowledge, always, the brilliant gold that marks all of us, not as flawed, but as human.

—L.P.
September 2020

TABLE OF CONTENTS

Philosophies, *1*
Ice in Fog, *3*
About Hurricanes, *4*
The Park, *5*
Familiarities, *7*
Where Stars Require No Wishes, *9*
Singularities, *11*
Circling the Periphery, *12*
Balancing Act, *14*
Always the Landing, *16*
40.6337N, 74.0909W, *18*
Memory of the Gust, *20*
Sounds, Strangers, and Shadows, *22*
No Use for Stars, *24*
Beautiful Lie, *26*
Gold, *28*
Expectation and Loss, *30*
Pages on Wind, *32*
I Don't Believe in Angels, *33*
Marco, *34*
The Summer of Your Dying, *36*
Counting Mondays, *38*
Winterizing, *40*
Slow Bend, *42*
Breaking the Bunny, *44*
The Loneliness of Folding a Sheet, *46*
Empty Road, *48*

Poem With No Periods, *50*
Autumn, Gathering, *52*
Wind, *54*
Standing Still, Being Still, *56*
Miles Down a Million Paths, *58*
Articulation, *60*
Softly Gone, *62*
Limitation of Lines, *63*
Playing Bocce, *65*
Cheap Buzzes, *67*
Empty Bottles, *68*
Basta, *70*
Between the Branch and the Wind, *72*
Hopeless Pursuits, *74*
Breadcrumbs, *76*
The Counter, *78*
Heavy with Light, *80*
Gardening, *82*
When Spring Returns, *84*
Behind Frost's Cabin, *86*
Ham and Eggs, *88*
The View from Here, *90*
Slice of Life, *92*
Chimney at Dusk, *94*
Inside the Glass, *96*
So Go the Decades, *98*
Balconies, *100*
Unmasked, *102*
In The Silence, Still, *104*

Philosophies

All the philosophies
wrestled to the floor in the night,
tamed like wild horses in the summer sun,
are there on pages like this.

What I believed in—
roads that led, inadvertently,
to unanticipated truths
alternates between momentary losses of faith
and returns to possibility.

I've sought revelations that might
make the cruelty of the world
and the people who inhabit it palatable,
willingly walled out and away
from what I couldn't fix.

My life's an open book
despite my efforts to keep it safely on a shelf.

Every philosophy I've donned and discarded,
all my contemplations about life,

come down to this:

Live it
as if you are always hungry.

Ice in Fog

We talk about time
as if we are not dying
when, in fact, life is terminal,
finite and dwindling.

No matter what the now,
the now is all I have,
spread across the pages of my life
like blue across familiar skies.

Across vast yesterdays,
love vanishes like water on wind,
dissipates like ice in fog;
tomorrow promises nothing.

There is today,
rainy, damp, and dreary
with the rhythm of poetry hitting my windows.
I am sure of only that
and of these words I woke up with
in the dark.

About Hurricanes

You worry about hurricanes—
water rising, breaking boundaries, flooding the world,
and washing us away in an instant;
gales of wind ripping things apart, shattering glass,
blowing through houses and scattering lives
across an ever-darkening sky;
sparks from downed power lines illuminating
empty streets and debris-filled shores
where, once, lovers strolled.

I smile, shake my head, and wonder
why you worry about hurricanes
when love is just as lethal and a more likely end.
It's fate, you see,
and if rising water breaks boundaries
and washes the world away, take comfort in this:

memory floats and is as good a life raft
as anything I can think of.

The Park

It's always red, this traffic light,
forcing me to stop beside the park
where we unwound many of our better days
before we unwound ourselves.

The girls loved it here,
and my arms remember the weight of lifting one
to grab the rings, repeatedly,
as she missed one and had to start again.
She squealed and did a victory dance
the day she finally made it all the way across.

The little one often sat inside the tube slide,
holding up traffic just because she could
and knew neither of us was climbing in to get her.
Eventually, a crankier child would push her out
and she'd cry as if none of it was her fault.

Before the light turns green,
I scan the space we occupied
and see the ghostly figures of those two little girls,
arms outstretched, running towards me,
shadow of you behind them on the bench,

shadow of me eclipsed by who I couldn't be,
then or now.

Familiarities
(For Paul)

Make no mistake,
these days are hard,
nights long with memories that break
on the shores of life as you knew it.

Forever altered, we are,
as the sky is every night
at the dying of the day,
bereft, even though
sunrise is a promise.

Some days, the emptiness will feel endless,
the roads behind you, a memory—
the road ahead winding and uncertain
as we wonder, perched on the present moment,
how we begin a life so void
of all our familiarities.

In the end,
the music inside will save you,
keep you tethered until you find the strength

to swim again,
just as my words have saved me from the depths,
loss after loss.

Remember this, if nothing else:
When sadness grabs you
and silence threatens to steal your soul,
music is often heard best
in empty spaces.

Where Stars Require No Wishes

Drawn to the sea,
I was tide to moon, magnetically pulled to shores,
the seagull's scream, reflection and release of my own
into the blue.

The poetry in the rhythmic thud of waves,
pounding like a heart,
was the pulse beneath my feet.

To get closer, I learned to sail
and rode the wind, mist in my face,
respectful of the water's power but unafraid
as darkness descended and the city rose
like Atlantis in the distance.
In that sacred moment and awesome silence,
I knew that this was where
I was meant to be.

Then, I stood on a lonely country road for the first time,
beneath a vaulting sky so alive with stars

it took my breath.
I heard, too, the poetry of water
sliding down rocks into clear pools and saw, there,
the reflection of the truest me I'd ever been
merge with clouds, also reflected there,
the closest to heaven I'd ever been.

I was drawn to the sea,
but born in the mountains
where Autumn comes soft and easy,
shadows dance across lavender skies
over still lakes at twilight,
and stars require no wishes.

Singularities

Oh, please! I say, mid-
conversation.
Don't bother me about love.
I know all I need to know.
Fire becomes ash swept into bins and tossed.
Candles only fool the darkness outside,
temporarily at best.
Been there. Done that. Learned this:
There's a reason why a shooting star's
a singularity.

Circling the Periphery

Do we choose the path
or does the path choose us?
Is my destiny written on the wind
or buried in some notebook I discarded
on my way to here?

All awakenings,
no matter what they seemed at the time,
were awakenings to myself,
sudden illumination in a dark moment
like some shadow struck a match
and I stuck my hand in the fire
to learn how to burn and be burned.

I've lived best at the edges,
circling the periphery
of love, laughter, loss,
in the margins, a life created
no other could touch, alter or break.

One either drowns
in the loneliness of being human
or drinks from it to nourish deeper places

than ordinary light can penetrate.

All the roads I've walked or failed to walk
were not accidents,
the paths I didn't choose
or those that didn't choose me
mere reckonings in a life of reckonings.

I am who I should be,
having learned not to put hand to fire
but pen to paper instead.

Balancing Act
(For Doreen)

Designs in splintering places,
the aging green wood would peel in strips
if pulled, and the heat from midday sun
radiated to the skin
as we sat at opposite ends.

See-saw, teeter-totter,
call it what you will.
It was the poetry of youthful motion and optimism,
one friend trusting the other to cushion hard landings,
strong legs pushing off the ground
or bending softly toward it to prevent collision.

Too young for metaphor,
we didn't see this simple thing reflected life—
its ups and downs,
its give and take,
the rise towards heaven,
the fall from grace.

In our own way,

we knew enough to strive for that moment
of total equilibrium, the moment of stasis
when the board between us remained absolutely level
as we achieved stillness,
the harmony of hearts necessary to create
that temporary perfection
only childhood allows.

It was always a balancing act.
It still is.

Always the Landing

On sweltering days,
hot metal burned the back of my legs
midway above the knee,
but I'd hop on anyway.

The ascent began,
a forward and backward quick step
followed by the rhythmic bend and stretch of the legs,
steady, continuous, necessary
for momentum and height.

It never took long to enter the blue
almost close enough to touch
but never close enough for me.
Never free enough in simple motion,
I needed more and so,
with timing perfected over time, I'd wait.
At the apex,
in that nanosecond
before the swing began its descent,
I'd launch myself into the air,
the arch of my young, healthy body hurtling,

without restraint or thought,
preparing itself, automatically,
for what was ahead.

It was always the landing I hated:
not the pain of feet slamming concrete,
but the loss of the sky,
the me I was in the air.

I learned too young what a moment can steal,
that even if I pumped those legs for a lifetime,
there'd always be a landing.

As children do,
I'd hop on anyway.

40.6337N, 74.0909W

I wear this on my wrist,
carved in ivory from Bali and in me
like that brook carved through rock
forging its path to vaster waters.
I didn't need to know its final destination,
only the part of the journey I'd witnessed.

Latitude and longitude,
places on a map or globe, navigation tools
for travelers or wanderers—
I need no tool to lead me to that place
between heaven, heartache, desire and despair.
I can find my way there in the dark.

The smell of rain, sound of leaves in the wind,
bright stars in an inky sky,
all live in my own dark spaces I keep safe
from a world that breaks things.

I wear this on my wrist
not to navigate but to articulate
memory that flickers
like a candle on the edge of the wind,

to remind myself of that precious,
fleeting time when

we were

we.

Memory of the Gust

Words. Snow.
Fall and melt into nothing
but traces of here and gone
like some tattered flag that retains
the memory of the gust that tore it.
I don't need to see the wind to know it blew.

Words. Leaves.
Fall from limbs that try
but cannot hold the sky;
it's a swirl of orange the eye follows
into a place beyond the eye
like that trail of color just after sunset.
I don't need to see the sun
to know it graced the sky.

Words. Tears.
Fall from unnamed places,
down unnamed faces,
joy and sorrow remarkably the same in expression.
I don't need to see tears to know they fell.

Words. Stars.
What I believe in, always,
when I raise my eyes to heaven, is not God;
it's the stars, whose existence,
firmly bolstered by science,
still gives rise to questions never meant
to be answered,
and unexpected poetry never meant
to be analyzed.

In the end, I will die before them,
and another poet,
perhaps not born yet,
will look up at a tattered flag,
recognize the memory of the gust and write—
Words.

Sounds, Strangers, and Shadows

That was the summer blood
stained the sidewalks of boroughs
suddenly too close for comfort,
a car's backfire enough reason to duck for cover,
nights of terror that robbed
simple acts of simplicity,
and a generation lost its innocence
to random violence.

On the music charts,
Rod Stewart and Andy Gibb;
on the front pages,
Son of Sam and kids whose only crime
was sitting in a car after dark.

We sat on the porch with heightened awareness
of sounds, strangers, and shadows,
the world a bit scarier, stars not enough light
to return our sense of safety.

In July, the city went dark,
all hell broke loose,
and the bloodied head of Stacy Moskowitz

became the symbol of a world gone mad.

Hard to believe that was the Summer,
43 years ago, now,
when Stacy was 20 and died,
and we listened to the baseball game on the radio
as if we could escape the fact
there was more in the dark than stars,
more in the world beyond the porch
than we ever needed or wanted to know.

No Use for Stars

I never walked that beach with you
in the silence after midnight,
the solitary sound of water lapping the shore.

You stood there, full orange moon on the bay
transforming the surface into fire,
and refused to walk with me.

I asked you to sit with me on the chair
two steps from the door you stood inside
to share the view and, again, you refused,
like there was some joy in denying the simplest
of my requests.

I lived too much inside myself, you told me,
was too attached to stars
and other things out of reach
and not enough to things at hand
(meaning you, I assumed).

My head, you said, was always in the stars
and I spent too much time
looking up to even see you

standing in front of me.

I did see you and wanted,
once, to give you that world outside the door,
but, apparently, you wanted a lover,
not a poet.

When all is said and done,
the reason for goodbye was far simpler
than you ever made it sound:

You had no use for stars,
and I couldn't live without *them*.

Beautiful Lie

It's not silence I remember;
it's words
whispered in the dark or wailed in the wind,
what others promised but failed to fulfill.

I listen to words the way most listen to music
and remember them the same way,
as songs I can sing, lyrics I can recite
years down the line.

Many words have failed me,
but never my own.
I recall those I've ridden on,
full of joy with the sound of them,
utterances that stole my breath away
for right and wrong reasons.

They'd run like scripts in my head,
if I allowed them,
the actors who spoke the lines
long gone from the stage of my life,
my recognition, even then,
that I was simply a fleeting chapter in a book

I did not want to write or read.

But in the dark,
I do not remember silence;
I remember words
and how beautiful a lie can sound
to a willing heart.

Gold

I visit the cemetery, lately,
half-heartedly and far removed from the person
who believed, once, you were watching over me
from a great height,
the way you did from the front porch windows.

Over 40 years gone, since that Saturday morning,
when a devastated sixteen-year old,
searched empty streets for something, anything
to cling to, your absence a chasm
I'd have gladly jumped into.
That moment taught me heartbreak,
and while I've known much worse since,
losing you defined me.

Keeping you close is like flying a kite
in October wind, and I cringe
when the thought of you escapes my grasp,
and I can recall your accent
but not the sound of your voice,
your smile but not the creases on your face.
By your headstone, I noticed trees
that never changed color

and died into bareness, instead.
I wiped the leaves from your grave,
saying aloud,
Well, I guess Frost was right, Gram.
Nothing Gold does stay, and you—
you were gold.

I smiled as I turned to go and saw,
there, on top of my shoe,
a solitary gold leaf.
Your way of re-defining leaving,
I suppose?

Expectation and Loss

Long ago, you gave me a piece of advice:
expect nothing, and you will
never be disappointed.

A fountain of wisdom,
I childishly believed you were,
even long after I knew better,
chalking up your harsh lessons
to love, friendship, that rare caring
I convinced myself we shared.

Then came that reckoning
when being true to you suddenly meant
betraying myself
in deeper places than I cared to contemplate.

When I stopped being your creation,
you had no use for me;
when the puppet ceases to respond
to the strings, it must go,
so I went.

My leaving did not diminish your life.

Angry at my refusal
to relinquish control to you again,
you never accepted that you were as guilty
of stealing my innocence as anyone else.

Designed to toughen me,
to wake me up,
your cruel wisdom accomplished its goal.

I walked away knowing I deserved more
than the nothing you expected me
to expect.

Pages on Wind

That line's not as distinct as one supposes—
that divides segments of time we've named
for referential or reverential reasons.
Does the color of day bleed into night
or does the color of night rise even in the setting?

Against a rippling sky, rippling water moves,
indifferent to human endeavor,
untold stories pocketed like coins
between small crests.

No coincidence
the descending day dies in orange,
harbinger of Autumn gathering
at the edges of my mind,
the technicolor goodbye that rises in me
like a tide and crashes on all my silent shores
or floats, softly,
pages on the winds of time
as it passes
and passes
and passes.

I Don't Believe in Angels

or that feathers I find are anything other
than remnants of birds,
memories of flight.

I do believe, though, in the spirit of the woods,
patches of blue sky visible through lines of poplars,
guardians of that world so devoid of this
it was like walking on another planet.

My breath, rising on cool mountain air,
infused every cell with vibration and freedom,
and I insensibly became me—
blood on fire with poetry as I took in
a vista as majestic as it was simple.

There is magic in shadows,
spirit guides in the spray of waterfalls
that whisper amid the roar and swirl below.

My religion's a birch,
my faith, or all I need of it,
encompassed in a red leaf floating downstream
on clear water by the side of the road.

Marco

Sweet summer afternoons,
the cool of the pool water
refreshing against oppressive heat.

On any given day, children wandered blindly
in the water,
hands outstretched, eyes closed,
ears like antennae searching for any sign
of a splash or gurgle to lead them
in the right direction.

Marco. . .Polo
Marco. . .Polo

a chant in the air,
a song of freedom and echo of life as we knew it
before we knew its realities.

I watch the children in the pool,
yard behind mine,
one floating on a raft, earpods in place,
another on the deck, texting like mad,
grateful I lived before inventions stole away

simple joys of simple sounds.

I am filled with the urge to shout
Marco,
but know I couldn't bear the silence after.

The Summer of Your Dying
(For Mom)

Blur of time, edges softened by sheer exhaustion,
from June to August, a passage
from anguish to acceptance, yours and mine,
of the inevitable end you met
so bravely.

Moments return, some like gifts,
others griefs.
Tired beyond tired,
in the end, it was the end of the endings,
with you, the death of all I knew.

I laid you to rest but still grapple
with the restlessness in me,
wondering if the blank page is full of promise
or just a blank page.

So much space around me and inside me,
it's like playing hide and seek with myself,
only I'm not looking as hard as I should be.

On the edge of my third season without you,
I hearken back to a year ago
and the Spring that ushered in
the Summer of your dying;
I pray to the universe that,
at the end of these longer days of light,
I will find my way back to me.

You found the courage to die on your terms;
may I find the courage, now, to live on mine.

Counting Mondays

Eventually, I'll stop counting Mondays,
cease saying today is the sixth, seventh, eighth
Monday you're gone.
Soon enough, it will slip my mind,
and I won't see 12:55 on the clock
and think of your final moment here.

I'll stop acknowledging each change of season
that passes without you,
the first Autumn you will not see,
the first new television season I'll watch
without the television so loud
one can hear it outside.

I'll stop grieving the loss of you
that happened before you actually died,
the slow slipping away of the mother I knew,
day by day,
the stranger you saw
when you looked in the mirror.

I'll forget how I rubbed your back,
traced your protruding bones

like a map back to my origins
and realized the truth is not in dying,
rather in living.

I entered the world and took my first breath
on a Monday, the 13th;
you exited the world and breathed your last
on a Monday, the 13th,
the circle now complete.

And eventually,
I will stop counting.

Winterizing

Small things bring reality home,
daily details of a life
continuously editing itself
into the shape of a new narrative.

Fact is, I've never been anything,
living in a perpetual state of becoming;
momentary, necessary transformations,
and all I know of forever
is it either exists in a single moment of memory
or not at all.

Cliché to say life is transient,
but also true, given we all die thousands of times
before we ever stop breathing and then,
well. . .damned if I know.

At the moment,
I've just removed the screen in the front door,
replacing it with the window
on this rainy, windy November morning,
thinking you were still here
when I did this switch in the Spring,

hoping for better days
I knew would not come.

But this, too, is necessary,
this winterizing,
different as it feels
in the absence of your voice.

Change of seasons,
indeed.

Slow Bend

But what is dead, really?

Absent from here and now,
perhaps present somewhere else;
a shedding of the skin for some incarnation
free of the shackles of physicality.

I think of the slow bend the body becomes,
a birch under too much ice,
misshapen by passing years,
strong but brittle like old bones.
The failure of the body's never been far from me,
others and my own,
a narrative of pain not to be rewritten,
only told the way it is.

But I have also witnessed
the beautiful dying of day,
the slow purple blend
of twilight sky descending,
the magnificent orange of leaves leaving,
colorful, profound,
silent in that passing season.

I've seen, too, skeletons
of thin, bare birches
stark white, nearly invisible
against frozen fields,
not ghosts but reminders
that another day will come,
and death, like life,
is but a moment in a line of moments,
mortal as flesh,
eternal as sky,
the slow bend of the soul
towards absolute selflessness.

Breaking the Bunny

It was a certifiable moment:
me, discoursing with a chocolate bunny
at the kitchen table.

This, the rabbit I bought you for Easter
on our final trip to the chocolate factory,
stood before me as testament to the addiction,
inherited from you.
No matter what, that trip
was imperative every year,
a tradition as sacred as the others.

And so, I sat at the table,
knowing it was time to break the bunny,
convincing myself I wouldn't
break into a million pieces with it.
I explained, to this inanimate thing,
the importance of the moment,
both a last and a first.

Then, I laid it down, slammed my fist down,
and felt it give way
and crumble under the weight

of my grief, my loss, a lifetime of
Easter-basket memories.

Never has chocolate tasted
so bitter
sweet.

The Loneliness of Folding a Sheet

Every day, a new discovery;
today, the loneliness of folding a sheet.

If there's a heaven and you're watching,
I'm sure you were all quite amused at the sight—
fitted Snoopy sheet in a ball on the bed,
me, sweaty, apple red-faced from the effort,
and furious that this seemingly simple task
seemed impossibly difficult.

Clearly, the inventor of the fitted sheet
was not alone.

I folded it this way, that way,
standing, sitting, draped it across the bed,
at one point wrapped like a mummy,
before I flung it on the bed
like some large Snoopy tumbleweed.

Catching my breath before the next round,
(because you know I do not give up),
I recognized this for what it was.

It was not about the sheet.
It was about the mother, the aunts, the grand-
mother
not here to hold the other end.
It was about surviving the missing you
that enveloped the moment.

I am happy to inform all of you
that the sheet is folded,
and I may damn well start sleeping
on a bare mattress.

Empty Road

(For Debbie)

An empty path vanishing into a bend,
trees bursting with autumn
reds, yellows, and oranges
on either side,
you call it your
Somewhere Down the Road photo.

I recall the day you snapped that shot—
upstate New York, after the rain.
You chased the scene,
waited for the light to perfect itself,
adjusted the camera and lens
what seemed a thousand times,
me behind you mumbling
that poetry was a hell of a lot faster.
In the end, of course,
I knew your patience and my aggravation
would look stunning in a wooden frame,
and so it does.

To you, that photo represents
the long-awaited something that never came,

the path that never led your heart home.

What I see is the mystery and possibility
of the road vanishing into a curve,
and though I know it leads to nowhere,
I smile anyway, grateful for the journey.

Every photo captures two moments—
the one inside the frame,
and the one outside.

Maybe that's all we need to know.

Poem With No Periods

Life seems like a run-on sentence
with one thing flowing into the other
without pause
without cause
and only memory for company:
tears flow, years fly,
hello comes, then goodbye,
and suddenly a moment's gone
before you had the chance
to feel it in your heart
where it will take residence
and haunt you like a smile you saw once
across a crowded room,
or the smell of cologne that reminds you
of a face you never touched
or the sunset you never shared
except in your mind—

and all of these become companions
on lonely summer nights
and hollow winter evenings
when even the heat of the fireplace
can't rid you

of the chill in your bones left behind,
not when love dies but when it fails to begin,
when love becomes a question with no answer
and you ask the question anyway only to discover
memory has no expiration date or time limit
when it lives in the heart,
that you will, against the odds,
love what you cannot have
until forever itself is a memoir—
period.

Autumn, Gathering

In the middle of Woodstock
sits a small park, one of many places
to bench yourself and absorb
the texture of Vermont
like paint on a canvas.

Not unusual to find there
painters with easels
furiously trying to capture
changing light on changing leaves,
photographers clicking the covered bridge
into permanence, impervious to weather,
or poets, like me,
contemplating the impossibility
of capturing this magic
in any medium.

The recollection is vivid—
how alive I was as I skittered, like a child,
ankle-high in golds, oranges,
and reds of a dying season.
This was Autumn, gathering at my feet,
and I picked up an armful of leaves,

gathering Autumn as if I could pull it
into my blood and keep it and that feeling
for another day.

Come to think of it,
maybe I have.

Wind

The sound of wind always leads me
to my room at the top of the world
where I *created* a world.

That room's a piece of a poem
I've been composing half my life now,
part of my story I can't adequately voice,
even today.

On the most beautiful nights of my life,
windows wide open,
the wind was a different song, every time,
I wrote lyrics to
with the joy of an unbroken heart.

The memory strikes now
like a distant clock
in the silence of summer air,
wind from the cross-breeze
passing above my prone body
on a particularly productive night.
My eyes fixed on starlight just outside,
I picked up the papers, flung them in the air

and made it rain poetry,
pages swirling around me
like the magic they were.

A lifetime removed,
heart worn and torn by life and loss,
I need to remind myself
that some rain requires no umbrella,
only faith.

Standing Still, Being Still

You don't learn stillness by watching
the dead; that's absence,
not presence.
Nothing to learn there.

You learn stillness
by observing a frozen lake,
listening to branches
crack beneath the weight of ice
until that rhythm
becomes your heartbeat.

You learn it, too,
beneath a gray winter sky
in the absence of signs of Spring,
recalling younger days when some force
compelled you to sit by the window
and understand life out there
and life in here
were worlds apart.

I learned to live inside,

out there being inhospitable
to my sensibilities,
chaos hostile to all things poetic.
Ages it took me to discover
standing still and being still are not the same,
one easy to achieve, the other a discipline.

I learned to be still by watching
a frozen lake beneath which my words, literally,
lived in suspended animation,
and, in the absence of sound,
learned to sing
the empty space and sky alive.

Miles Down a Million Paths

The roads I've walked,
I've walked alone by both necessity and choice,
story of my life a continuous game
of hide-and-seek with myself.

What's down on pages pales
compared to what's not—
so many times on the precipice of expression,
I chose silence instead,
safe and stifling.

I can't explain me even to me,
except to say
I surrendered to the truth long ago,
by far, my best and loneliest moment.

Love, perhaps, shouldn't ask of one
the impossible, yet here I am,
miles down a million paths
that still lead to where I started.

In the end,
the joy, the pain, desire, and despair

are testament enough.

Nothing to hide.
Nothing to seek, either.

Articulation

(For Jerri)

I never forget a kindness
and, from you, have known many.

Over thirty years, give or take,
in twenty-minute intervals,
you've come to know me better
than people I've wasted countless hours with,
a lesson there about compression
of time and the art of true listening.

In snippets, we've shared
laughter and loss,
hope and heartache,
advice and authenticity,
commonalities and connection
built over a long succession of moments,
an accomplishment in a divided universe.

Faithless though I am,
you've often managed to restore some
with a simple, offhand comment
or piece of advice,

delivered with compassion and a smile.

I think you read me
long before you read me,
the words on the pages merely proof
of what you knew was there, in me,
because you took the time to look.

We are both, you see,
experts at adjusting,
masters of articulation,
and you, whether you know it or not,
have (beyond the literal sense)
kept my head on my shoulders
more times than I can count
in all the ways that matter.

Softly Gone

Whisper of an autumn breeze,
memory of a hand touching your face;
leaf floating on wind,
memory of dreams falling from the heavens;
rain tapping on the roof,
music different from any song written
by human hands:

softly, like sinking into the arms of love,
falling into eyes that speak without words,
memory of the all in all
became nothing but the memory of someone
softly leaving the room,
leaving the poem,
softly gone
but gone.

Limitation of Lines

In kindergarten,
Sister Elizabeth beat my knuckles
nearly bloody with a ruler
for sloppy penmanship.

My five-year-old brain,
on fire like my hand,
knew this would teach me nothing;
writing seldom improves
when you can't bend your fingers.

I couldn't stay on the line
was the thing, or maybe I did not like
the limitations of the lines
on the page, my ideas fenced in,
not free to venture past
what someone else would think acceptable.

Truthfully, I feared Sister Elizabeth
more than the God I was supposed to believe in,
sure, if he existed, that he didn't care
about my sloppy writing,
either way.

A lifetime away,
I recall the ache of my hands,
knuckles red against the white page,
when, she said,
"*How much is left
if you take five away from five?*"
and I scribbled, in absolute defiance,
one word, slanted to the right:
Nun.

I don't think I even tried to stay on the line.

Playing Bocce

(For John, and all the indelible moments like this one)

Some memories slip quietly into thought
and take up residence
in empty corners of yourself.
Others fall heavier, a thud in the night,
startling and as sudden as a smile.

You sat there, one summer afternoon,
curly-haired cute, back against the black,
wrought-iron rail on the porch
where so much of life played itself out.

The banter was funny, air resounding with laughter
and the cacophony of kids playing in the side yard.
Then, you spied them,
a worn set of bocce balls in the silver milk box.

You lifted one, noting it was heavier than it looked,
and threw it in the air, catching it on the way down,
ignored repeated warnings
about what might happen—until it did.

A throw went awry,

the bocce ball clanged on the railing
before bouncing on your head
with a clunk.

You spewed some choice words,
accused the one who'd warned you
of being a witch,
then asked for an aspirin.

Years away,
I recall the amazing vista of stars
afforded us from that porch
and smile at how you gave seeing stars
and entirely new meaning.

Cheap Buzzes

Sweet, sticky liquid oblivion
we chugged in woods and darkened
parking lots, away from the eyes of the world.

Radio blaring,
summer nights shattered by rock music
that nearly shook stars loose,
we sipped the night away
dreaming when dreams were a dime a dozen
and we had dozens of dimes to spare:

Boone's Farm, Tango,
Pink Champale, Grape Duck—
the sweet, sticky tasty of youth
in search of something more that was only more
than it was cracked up to be,

those cheap buzzes
suddenly more priceless
than we ever imagined they would be.

Empty Bottles

They punctuated the end of every summer night,
empty bottles strewn across the ground,
remnants of the good time
we'd have a bad time with
at daybreak.

No regrets amid the trash,
just memories of the sip-and-kiss stupidity
of kids in dire need of adventure.

Back then, I counted stars twinkling
at the bottom of the beer I drank
to obliviate myself.
No one knew the places I went,
how far away I was,
head back, eyes closed—gone,
just gone

like the beer,
like the bottle I smashed against the rock.

After all this time,
I see now what I didn't then.

Those bottles weren't the only things empty
at the end of the night,
the difference between trash and trashed
not as clear as one might believe.

Basta

(For Grandma)

Here they are again,
the words that find me every year
when days darken early and the past is too close
to escape.

The air feels heavy with a grief,
barely remembered, the sky streaked with red
like the scar I carry inside.

I am here,
39 Octobers come and gone,
since last I saw kind eyes whose love
I never questioned.

There is so little kindness in anyone these days;
I ache for the simple language we spoke
on rainy afternoons at the kitchen table
where I tried to teach you to play cards,
a futile but funny endeavor
given you could not read numbers
or tell a king from a jack.

I laugh, recalling the string
of Italian words sliding off your tongue
in frustration, hand motions to match,
as you rose and said, *"Basta"*!

39 Octobers later, I'd double down on all of it
for one more afternoon,
one more chance to say my time with you
was not *"Basta"*—
not even close.

Between the Branch and the Wind

This is the silence that falls to silence,
leaves to the ground, suddenly, out of nowhere;
one minute part of the tree,
the next of the nothingness that follows.

Funny how that happens,
the unexpected but necessary letting go
of something you weren't thinking of
but whose absence you suddenly feel
like a hollow opened inside
and all you hear is echo.

I think of you that way,
as echo and reverberation,
as something that left in the night
without word or warning.
There in the moonlight,
gone by daybreak,
me wondering if it was a dream,
knowing it wasn't.

Lying here in the silence that falls to silence,
I find myself

between the branch and the wind,
not quite part of the tree,
or of the nothingness either.

Hopeless Pursuits

Once, I was limitless
and dreams, weightless things,
floated over me like ribbons in the wind.
I was content to watch the poetry of motion,
indifferent to the dream escaping me.

When you are infinite,
the parameters of days folding into nights
mean little;
one lives in the immediate now of now
with no hindsight, foresight, or regrets.

I lost the best of me
when I stopped lying in the grass and staring
into the glittering universe
because it suddenly felt out of reach,
a hopeless pursuit.

Years later,
all grown up, I stood beneath the vaulting heaven
of a Vermont sky on some darkened back road
and re-discovered my truth—
the only hopeless pursuit

is the one we abandon
to what the world wants us to be.

I have been limitless ever since.

Breadcrumbs

I barely recall drunkenness,
that particular dizziness, a wisp of hair in the wind,
flitting, thin, hard to grasp.

But I do remember hot breath on winter air,
frozen ground beneath my back,
hard like stone, even through my parka,
the way cold seeped through my Levi's
and into my thighs as I lay there
in a silent world searching for words
to describe the stars.

Cliché after cliché,
such trite comparisons I daren't write them
even here.
Then, suddenly, words appeared
like visitors at the door to my soul:

"The stars," I said aloud,
*"are the breadcrumbs poets scatter
to light their way home."*
It was a good moment's reward

and I scribbled that line
on the bottom of my sneaker
and limped to my door not to lose it.

Those stars are summoning me
these days, and I should heed the call,
if for nothing else
than to remind myself that there are
better reasons than brokenness and pain
to limp home.

The Counter

Every Saturday, up early,
I'd await my trip to the beauty shop.

Sure, the lovely ladies would make a fuss—
ply me with candy, allow me to play
with the rollers,
but that was prologue to the best part of the day,
when, dolled up and smiling,
my aunt would zip my jacket and take my hand.
My heart beat with excitement
as we crossed the street, hand in hand,
and walked the cracked sidewalks
to the Five and Dime.
Front windows alive with the shiny stuff
kids love, Woolworth's towered on the burgundy
awning above them.

In we'd go, aisle to aisle,
and she'd get me anything I wanted,
though I never wanted much.

Then, we'd sit at the lunch counter

on, round, revolving, red
faux-leather seats and order fries.
I still hear the scratch of the plate
riding the laminate as Ned-with-the-green-eyes
(for years, I thought that was his name)
shouted, *"Ready, kid?"* and slid it down
for me to catch.

All gone now, the Five and Dime,
my aunt,
the child I was on all those Saturdays.

Part of me's still at the counter, though,
wondering how much a memory goes for,
how much of my childhood I could buy for a dime
if, for a plugged nickel, my aunt could get me
anything my heart desires.

These days, I want a lot more.

Heavy with Light

I need a transfusion of green
in ways I can't articulate;
to see your beautiful rising against the sky,
lavender twilight bleeding into purple nights.

My eyes hunger for you
like someone awaiting a lover after long absence.
Memorized as you are,
recollection isn't enough, and I ache
to smell balsam in the autumn night air,
to feel the planks of a covered bridge
creak beneath my feet,
what I can glimpse through the lattice
all the world I need.

I crave the music of a brook,
suddenly there, in the middle of nowhere,
constant reminder
that softness cuts through stone
and forges a path of infinite possibility.

I long for the artistry,
shadows of clouds painting mountains

as day disappears into the magic of stars
so profuse the sky feels heavy with light.

Oh, Vermont.
I'm not waiting for you to call me home
I'm waiting for *me* to call *you* home.

Gardening

My grandmother could plant a rock and from it,
grow a tree;
my mother, the same.
I did not inherit this gift.

In fact,
I can and have killed even plants
deemed unkillable,
not from cruelty or indifference,
simply from negligence of faith
that it could be any other way.

My thumbs were never green,
colored instead with a rainbow of inks
that slipped out of the fountain pens
that watered my words and what grew there,
on empty pages, through all my ages.

Paper comes from trees,
and from those trees and on those trees
I have written an Eden,
a heaven and a hell,
paradise found and lost.

I've dirtied my hands
with far more permanent stuff than soil,
cultivated gardens,
grown poems from all the rocks
life has thrown in my face.
I have always preferred
blue skies to green thumbs,
no matter my heritage.

When Spring Returns

Eyes to the sky, I waited in the car
and skeletal bare limbs reminded me
everything here is dead—
all the people beneath
or behind stone inscriptions,
all the trees that surround them.

The silence of this place,
astoundingly peaceful, is far removed
from the noise and stresses of survival,
not lonely but lonesome.

I got familiar with this place
far too well, far too young,
though it's changed over time,
a house continuously annexed
to accommodate a growing family.

I drive narrow streets between graves by heart,
glad I memorized them, since no one's here
to guide me.

Strange that a cemetery

feels like home, but it does,
so many parts of me here.

Instantly, the sky behind those skeletal trees
turned deep crimson and orange
as it might on a summer evening,
not at Winter Solstice,
the shortest day of the year.

When Spring returns,
those trees will green, the blossoming reminder
of memory's endurance
in a place where everything is dead—-
and nothing is.

Behind Frost's Cabin

is a deep dark woods, poplars
shooting so far into the sky
it's dizzying to look up.

In another lifetime,
we walked there, two souls,
not in search of
but discovering, instead,
things we couldn't articulate in words
or capture with a click.

The snap, snap, snapping of twigs
beneath my boots was the rhythm of the moment,
the click, click, clicking of your camera,
counter-beat.

I leaned against a tree,
watched you on the ground,
working your magic, as a ray of orange light
pierced the space between the trees
lighting up the edges of your face.

I return, in my mind,

to the cool of a forest with little sun,
the miracles in the shadows there,
the memory of another poet who walked there
and fell in love, as did I,
with the dizziness of looking up
and glimpsing in the treetops
a trace of heaven.

Ham and Eggs

Rituals:
familiar repetitions we can trust,
stability in a world that is anything but.

The measures of my life with you became,
by necessity, beats on a metronome,
a rhythm that kept chaos
just outside the perimeter.

I sank comfortably into the life
defined, largely,
by the needs of others,
simply because if I didn't,
joy would have escaped me completely,
and that, I couldn't live with.

My defining moment came
when I sat beside your still-warm body,
placed my hand on your unbeating heart
and realized that your last breath
and my first breath, after, were intertwined.

Nearly a year since then,

I recall all the rituals
of our companionship,
all I've had to become
and unbecome in my life.

Right now, I'm cooking ham and eggs,
like I did every Friday after the beauty shop;
for the life of me, Mom,
I cannot decide if this feeling is freedom
or desolation.

The View from Here

Countless the times I sat in this chair,
ears so attuned to your movements
I knew you were up before my eyes
spied you.

In the fading light of day slipping
between blind slats,
I still see your stooped figure,
holding the cedar chest for guidance,
shadow of your former self, close behind,
haunting you like a ghost.

Day after day, for so long,
I'd contemplate, as you slept,
what it would be like
when you didn't wake up.
Then, you didn't.

I still can't say what it's like,
if it's how I'd imagined
in all those empty hours.

I do know, as I sit in this chair,

the view from here is the same,
and when my eyes move
in the direction of your room,
I am struck dumb
by the realization of your absence
from the space you occupied
in this house,
in my life.

Slice of Life

There are stories here,
slice-of-life narratives by the hundreds
in a space no larger than a book.
That's what I think as I hold
your small blue cutting board in my hands.

No way to count the times
you sat at this table,
dicing, slicing, chopping
what would, magically,
become a meal—
not a talent I inherited,
judging by my diet these days.

I trace the long cuts in the board
with my fingertips,
like remnants of suicide scars,
parts of my history written, not by me,
but you.

I read between the lines, the story
of all the mouths you fed,
holiday feasts, birthday parties,

and the simple daily meals
that nourished us and all began here,
on this little cutting board.

The final things you sliced were carrots
for the chicken soup we made, together,
in the weeks before your death.

You always said you should write a book,
never realizing you actually had,
and as I pick up where you left off,
I realize that the first cut is not the deepest.
The last is.

Chimney at Dusk

Perfect scene—
red house in the distance,
smoke rising from the chimney
into a wintry sky at dusk,
brook half-frozen,
surrounded by a landscape white
with fresh snow.

My eyes stare at this knowing it is real,
though it looks like
some Currier and Ives moment
that fills the heart with longing too deep
for mere words.

I imagine the roaring
responsible for the smoke
curling toward the heavens,
the orange glow
in back windows I can't see.

I think about who might be
sharing this moment,
the comfortable conversation

between the walls I'm outside of,
who is inside living the life
I've only lived inside my head for so long.

The snow is blank—
page without words,
canvas without paint,
face without feeling,
mind without memory.

I'm only a ghost here,
and ghosts leave no footprints.

Will I ever, I wonder,
step out of myself and into the life
I was meant to live?
Will the smoke ever
belong to me?

Inside the Glass

So much of my life's
about windows and the world
just outside them
for as long as I can remember,
my hand pressed to the glass.

Countless the times I imagined
shattering air as I punched a hole in the sky
so I could climb out of here and into
who knows what or where.

Then, I realized what I sought
was not out there but was inside the glass,
in the eyes reflecting back at me,
the one heart I could trust.

Looking out tonight,
foreground of darkness, light behind,
I saw, over my shoulder, the reflection
of myself at 13.

This world and hers, nowhere near the same,
yet what we see and feel

is the familiar loneliness
of a singular faith in the stars.

I turn, in silence,
from the reflection in the glass
to the shadow beside me and smile
as 13 meets 59 in an instant
of truth and recognition:

it is the same heart that beats inside,
the same hand pressed to the glass,
not to touch the world
but to keep it out.

So Go the Decades

So go the decades cascading
like dominoes into the final silence
of change.

We marvel at time's simultaneity,
the lightning speed of dreams
transitioning into memories,
slow dances of days unfolding into years,
all the while knowing time's the one thing
we cannot escape without transcending
life itself.

To look behind with joy is a joy;
to look ahead with hope, a gift,
faith that there's promise in the unknown
and light in dark corners if we seek it.

On the precipice of tomorrow
choices fall like confetti,
dreams of the world visible
on the breath of those who count down
to a midnight that changes nothing
but the date.

As for me,
for whom numbers mean nothing,
I intend to shake out
the dark blanket of sky,
let the stars rain down
and ride their light
into a tomorrow different from today.

There are more ways
to transcend life than by simply dying,
and dominoes only cascade
if someone unafraid of the falling
makes the first move.

Balconies

Faraway place,
streets my grandparents walked before
they were Grandma and Grandpa,
roots of a tree I've never climbed.

Only in photos or films
have I seen cobblestone streets
no wider than alleys,
buildings on either side, anchors
for clotheslines stretched across,
white shirts fluttering in the breeze
like the wings of angels.

I imagine simultaneity of one voice
fading into another in the early morning,
one-hundred-part harmony,
hands rising and falling,
words accentuated in ways one understands
without speaking the language.

The simplicity of it returns me
to a childhood moment,
when the smell of espresso

filled the house, wafted through the screen
and into the yard where I sat
listening to the lilt
of my mom and grandma conversing.

Watching the news, tonight,
streets emptied by fear,
I heard the rise of voices, one by one,
singing to the heavens, music overtaking
the silence of the dying nearby,
filling the skies with light
in the midst of profound sorrow,
*"I heard there was a secret chord,
David played and it pleased the Lord. . . ."*

Tonight, I understood
why Italy has so many balconies.

Unmasked

People—
they steal the poetry right from my pen
with their stupidity.

I'm offended by those offended
by any thought divergent from theirs,
who strive to silence any voice
that sings a different tune and claim
their rights are violated by mine
to live.

Now, it's the masks,
the ignorance and indifference
of not-so-human beings
unashamed of their selfish refusal
to protect others.

Part of me is amused at their refusal,
and it takes great restraint
to keep to myself, this:

You complain as if you haven't worn a mask
most of your life;

only difference is this one's visible.

People—
they steal the poetry.

In The Silence, Still

> "*A billion stars go spinning through the night,
> glittering above your head,
> But in you is the presence that will be
> when all the stars are dead.*"
> —Rainer Maria Rilke

These empty streets tell a story; void
of traffic and noise,
in the silence,
the echoing memory of life
reverberates in hollow spaces.

A stranger stops, mid-step, and looks at me—
the shell-shocked, blank stare of a soldier
who never committed to this fight.
He knows, now, what the poets have always known,
how tenuous the thread that binds us
to the world and to each other really is;
that those who can, throw stars into the darkness
to fill it with some necessary light,
that those who can't, tear it to shreds, then blame
the sky for falling on their heads—
not enough of one,

too many of the other.

Before is already gone,
after yet to come.
Rest assured, that every "new normal"
is simply a variation of something
lost and irretrievable.

What we learn depends
on who we are
and who we become in that stunning moment
when, stripped of all our illusions,
as we have been, right now,
we face ourselves in the mirror.

For tonight, it's enough to watch the day sink
into magnificent red and acknowledge
the quivering simultaneity
of profound sorrow and translucent hope
in the silence,
still

Alphabetical Index of Titles

40.6337N, 74.0909W, *18*
About Hurricanes, *4*
Always the Landing, *16*
Articulation, *60*
Autumn, Gathering, *52*
Balancing Act, *14*
Balconies, *100*
Basta, *70*
Beautiful Lie, *26*
Behind Frost's Cabin, *86*
Between the Branch and the Wind, *72*
Breadcrumbs, *76*
Breaking the Bunny, *44*
Cheap Buzzes, *67*
Chimney at Dusk, *94*
Circling the Periphery, *12*
Counting Mondays, *38*
Empty Bottles, *68*
Empty Road, *48*
Expectation and Loss, *30*
Familiarities, *7*
Gardening, *82*
Gold, *28*
Ham and Eggs, *88*
Heavy with Light, *80*
Hopeless Pursuits, *74*
I Don't Believe in Angels, *33*

Ice in Fog, *3*
In The Silence, Still, *104*
Inside the Glass, *96*
Limitation of Lines, *63*
Marco, *34*
Memory of the Gust, *20*
Miles Down a Million Paths, *58*
No Use for Stars, *24*
Pages on Wind, *32*
Philosophies, *1*
Playing Bocce, *65*
Poem With No Periods, *50*
Singularities, *11*
Slice of Life, *92*
Slow Bend, *42*
So Go the Decades, *98*
Softly Gone, *62*
Sounds, Strangers, and Shadows, *22*
Standing Still, Being Still, *56*
The Counter, *78*
The Loneliness of Folding a Sheet, *46*
The Park, *5*
The Summer of Your Dying, *36*
The View from Here, *90*
Unmasked, *102*
When Spring Returns, *84*
Where Stars Require No Wishes, *9*
Wind, *54*
Winterizing, *40*

ABOUT THE AUTHOR

Linda Principe is an adjunct professor of English at the College of Staten Island, where she has taught writing and literature for the last thirty-three years. A freelance writer and editor, she is the author of *Surviving Murder: A True-Crime Memoir*, which recounts the harrowing murders of of her aunt and uncle by their son, and two previous volumes of poetry, *Tangible Remains: Selected Poems,* and *Echoes of Light: New Poems.* Writing poetry since the age of thirteen, her poems have appeared, through the years, in a variety of publications. In her spare time, she enjoys reading, playing the guitar, songwriting, and collecting sea glass.

www.ingramcontent.com/pod-product-compliance
Lightning Source LLC
Chambersburg PA
CBHW022120040426
42450CB00006B/774